I Love Horses

Arabians

Maria Koran

AV2

www.av2books.com

Step 1
Go to **www.av2books.com**

Step 2
Enter this unique code
LHEGTG2BO

Step 3
Explore your interactive eBook!

AV2
I Love Horses
Arabians
Start!

AV2 is optimized for use on any device

Your interactive eBook comes with...

Audio
Listen to the entire book read aloud

Videos
Watch informative video clips

Weblinks
Gain additional information for research

Try This!
Complete activities and hands-on experiments

Key Words
Study vocabulary, and complete a matching word activity

Quizzes
Test your knowledge

Slideshows
View images and captions

View new titles and product videos at www.av2books.com

Arabians

CONTENTS

2 AV2 Book Code
4 Arabians
6 Bodies
8 Coats and Colors
10 Personality
12 Working
14 Foals
16 Where They Come From
18 Horse History
20 Modern Arabians
22 Know Your Horses
24 Key Words

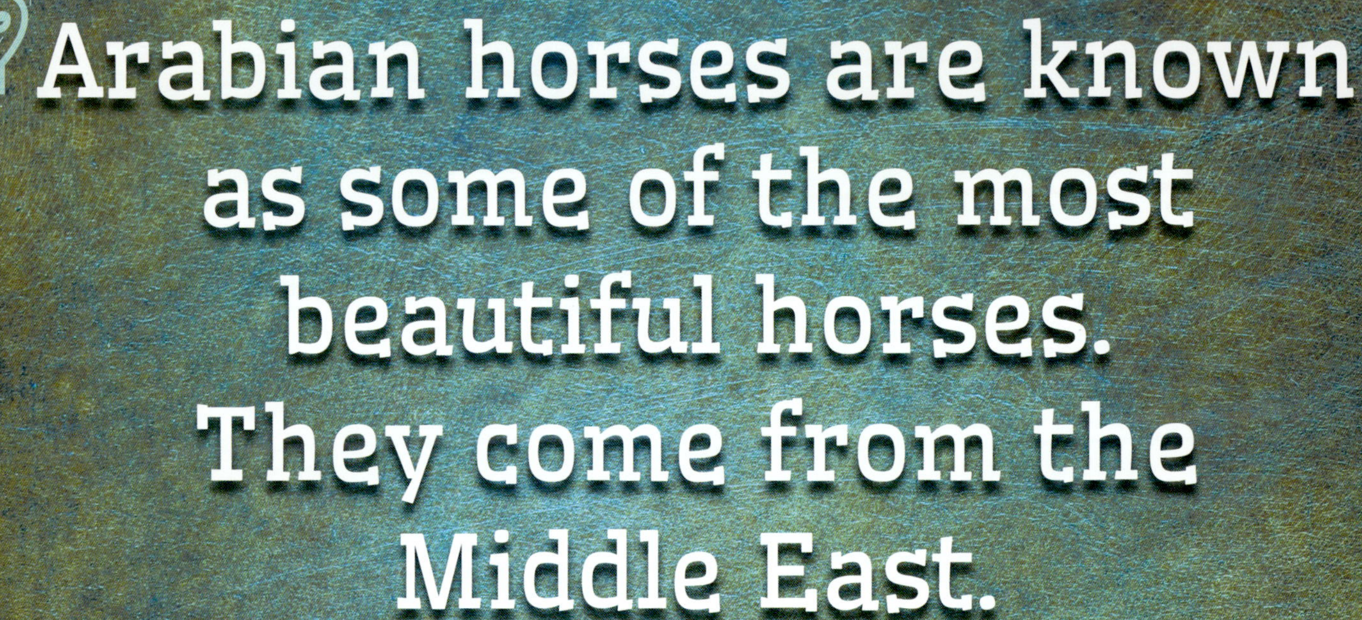

Arabian horses are known as some of the most beautiful horses. They come from the Middle East.

Arabian horses first came to the United States in 1725.

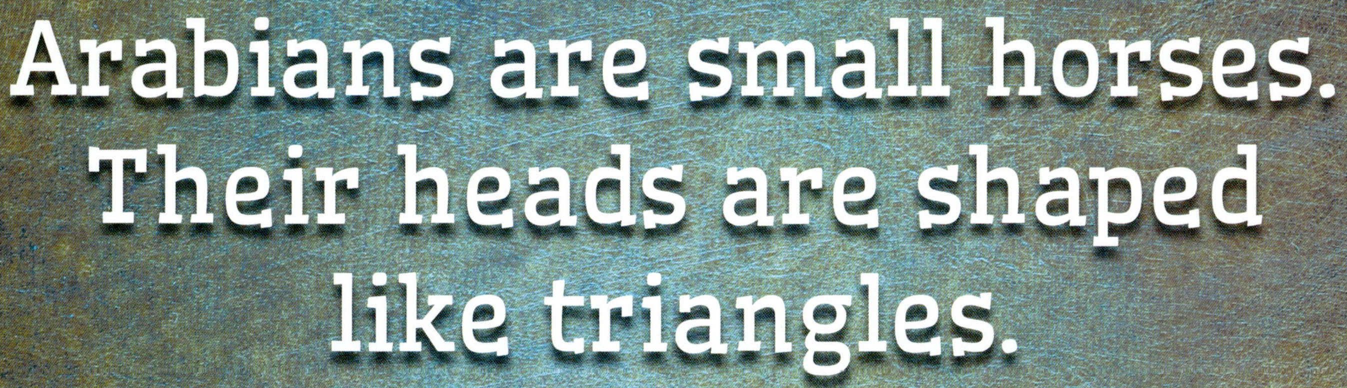

Arabians are small horses. Their heads are shaped like triangles.

Arabians have long manes and tails.

Most Arabians have coats with just one color.

They are often brown or gray. Some Arabians are black or white.

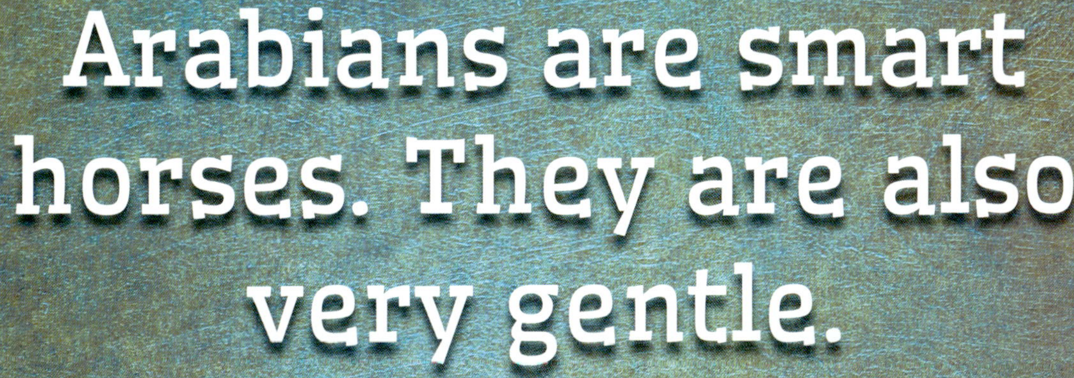

Arabians are smart horses. They are also very gentle.

Arabians are good horses for children and families.

People ride Arabians in endurance races. These races last for days.

Arabians can race up to 100 miles (161 kilometers) each day.

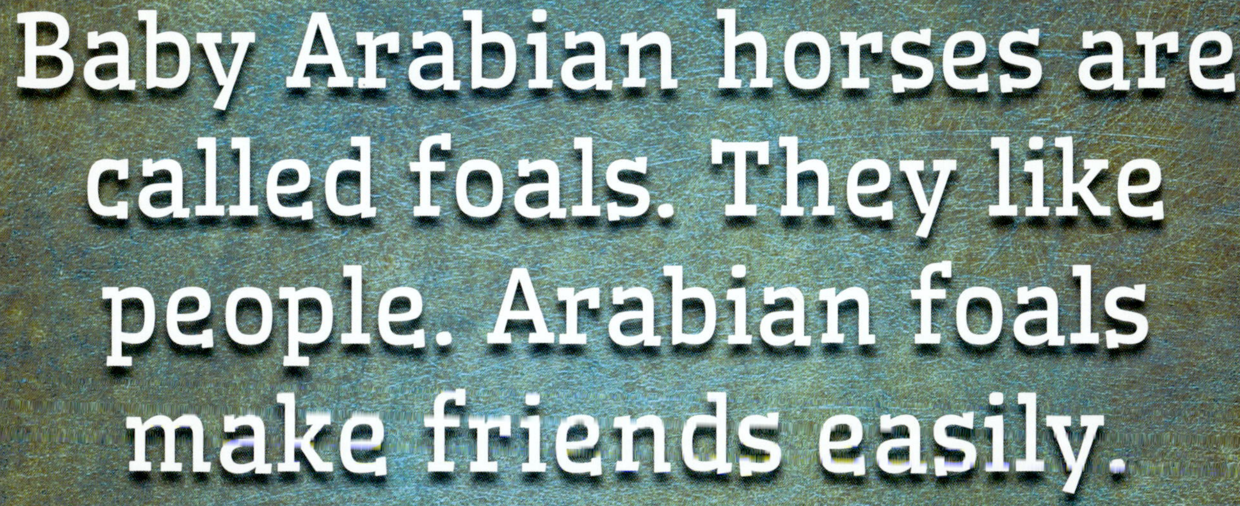

Baby Arabian horses are called foals. They like people. Arabian foals make friends easily.

Arabian foals stay with their mothers for about six months.

Arabians came from Middle Eastern war horses.

The horses had to be fast and smart. Their riders never stayed in one place for long.

People in Europe liked these horses, too.

They started to ride them. Then, Arabians came to North America as well.

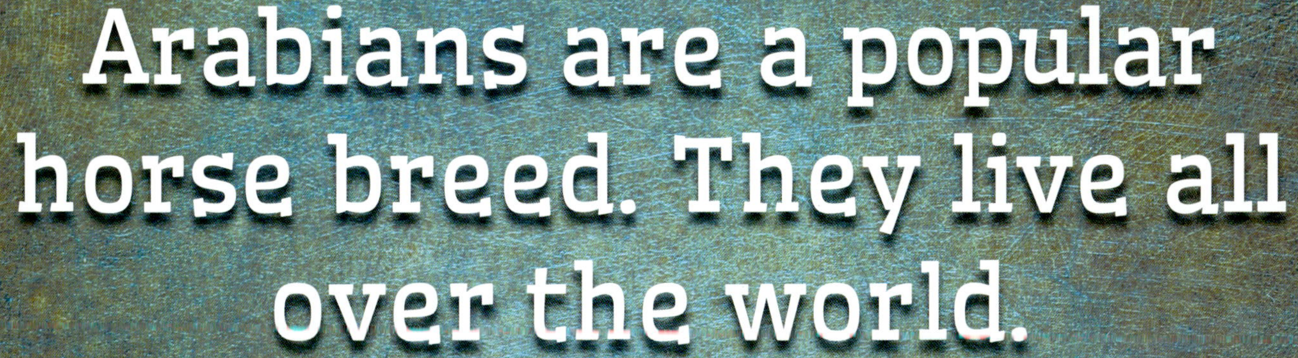
Arabians are a popular horse breed. They live all over the world.

Today, most Arabian horses are in the United States.

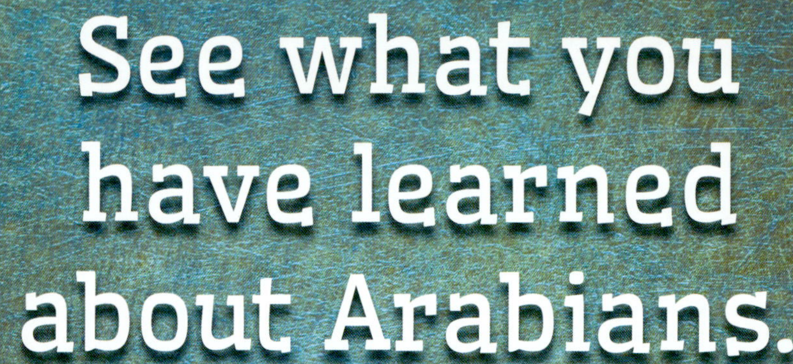

See what you have learned about Arabians.

Which of these pictures show Arabians?

KEY WORDS

Research has shown that as much as 65 percent of all written material published in English is made up of 300 words. These 300 words cannot be taught using pictures or learned by sounding them out. They must be recognized by sight. This book contains 55 common sight words to help young readers improve their reading fluency and comprehension. This book also teaches young readers several important content words, such as proper nouns. These words are paired with pictures to aid in learning and improve understanding.

Page	Sight Words First Appearance
4	are, as, came, come, first, from, in, known, most, of, some, the, they, to
7	and, have, heads, like, long, small, their
8	just, often, one, or, white, with
11	also, children, for, good, very
12	can, days, each, last, miles, people, these, up
15	about, make, mothers
16	be, had, never, place
18	too
19	started, them, then, well
21	all, over, world

Page	Content Words First Appearance
4	Arabian horses, horses, Middle East, United States
7	manes, tails, triangles
8	coats, color
11	families
12	endurance races
15	foals, friends, months
16	riders, war horses
18	Europe
19	North America
21	breeds

Published by AV2
350 5th Avenue, 59th Floor New York, NY 10118
Website: www.av2books.com

Copyright ©2021 AV2
All rights reserved. No part of this publication may be reproduced, stored in a retrieval system, or transmitted in any form or by any means, electronic, mechanical, photocopying, recording, or otherwise, without the prior written permission of the publisher.

Library of Congress Control Number: 2019955056

ISBN 978-1-7911-1951-5 (hardcover)
ISBN 978-1-7911-1952-2 (softcover)
ISBN 978-1-7911-1953-9 (multi-user eBook)
ISBN 978-1-7911-1954-6 (single-user eBook)

Printed in Guangzhou, China
1 2 3 4 5 6 7 8 9 0 24 23 22 21 20

022020
100919

Project Coordinator: John Willis Art Director: Terry Paulhus

AV2 acknowledges Alamy, iStock, Minden Pictures, and Shutterstock as the primary image suppliers for this title.